The Recession Will Make You Rich

How to Invest During a Recession

Table of Contents

Introduction

Ask anyone, and they will agree that recessions can hit you hard. It is difficult to continue living the lifestyle you have always enjoyed during the recession. It can even become difficult to fulfill your basic necessities during a recession. But what if someone were to tell you that instead of losing money during the recession, you can invest in such a way that you will end up benefiting from the cash crunch?

This book will serve as a guide for everyone who wants to earn profits during a recession. It will teach you how to invest during the recession, allowing you to gain great wealth with little to no effort. A recession will prove to be a once-in-a-lifetime opportunity for you!

There are certain things that you must remember while you try to earn profits during a recession. You cannot earn more money if you do not have any cash at hand. This means you need some capital to invest if you want to gain profits during a recession. This capital will be invested for a long time, as it is difficult to time the rock bottom of a market crash.

The market is always volatile but becomes even more volatile during a recession. You must have seen countless news articles about big, small, and medium-level companies filing for bankruptcy during a recession. While the number of medium and small companies filing for bankruptcy during a recession is generally high, big companies often sail through with a few battle wounds only. It is thus recommended to stick to the big guns and invest only in big companies during a recession.

Make sure that these companies will not tank or fail. Try to locate companies that continue to make money even at a low valuation. You will incur heavy losses if you try to support small companies during this time.

This book will teach you how to find safe companies and how you can invest in them. A recession can be hell for even big companies, but if you invest well, you will not only sail through this difficult time, but you may even end up earning lots of profit.

In this book, you will also learn about dollar cost averaging and various strategies you can follow to get a good profit at the end of the recession. The numbers may seem dwindling dangerously now, but trust your game and investment and play it safe. Do not try to be excessively optimistic about earning huge profits by investing huge sums. It is better to start slow. Do not put all your eggs in one basket as you are found to lose a lot of money this way.

I want to thank you for choosing this book, and I hope it will help you make loads of money in this difficult time.

Chapter One: Always Have Hard Cash

One of the first things you need to understand about investing in a recession is what a recession is. They are a period when the GDP sees a significant decline for more than two quarters. It is an unfortunate condition that may create a lot of problems for people all around the world.

The market becomes extremely volatile during a recession, leading to losses left, right, and center. But this does not mean that you still cannot make profits during a recession. The only thing you need to make more money is money itself.

What Is a Recession?

A recession can be defined as the downward movement of the GDP or the gross domestic product for two or more consecutive quarters. According to the National Bureau of Economic Research, NBER, during a recession, there is a significant decline in economic activity that is widespread and lasts for many months. A recession can negatively affect GDP, employment, retail, and wholesale sales. It can also bring down real income.

What Are the Causes of Recessions?

In the past, there have been multiple issues that have caused recessions. However, most of them have occurred due to economic imbalances that had to later be corrected. For instance, the excess housing market debt was the main reason behind the 2008 recession. The rise of technology stocks was the cause of the 2001 recession.

Other than these reasons, a sudden and drastic change in the world can also lead to inflation. For instance, the COVID-19 pandemic led to a period of recession.

A recession is often characterized by unemployment. When people lose jobs, or there is a lot less hiring, people tend to have a reduced spending capacity and will. This increases the pressure on the economy and affects company earnings and stocks. These factors create a dangerous cycle that may destroy the economy.

Recessions are painful experiences, but this does not mean we can or should always try to avoid them. Recessions are natural and necessary as they allow for the clean-up of the excesses so that the economy can be fresh and ready for the next economic expansion.

How Long Do Recessions Last?

A good thing about recessions is that they generally do not last long. Generally, a recession can last between two to 18 months, on average ten months. Granted, this period may seem like eons to people who have either lost their jobs or do not have one. It can be daunting and stressful for businesses on the verge of closing. But a recession could be a boon for investors who are happy to invest for the longer term.

Recessions are generally a tiny blip in the history of economics. The net economic impact of recessions is not much high.

What Happens to the Stock Market During a Recession?

It is difficult to predict a recession's onset, peak, and decline, but it is recommended to be ready for it. Bear markets tend to overlap with an economic decline. Here the equities may lead by almost seven months at the top and bottom of the cycle.

Equities generally go up a few months before the recession but may fall rapidly. However, any aggressive and haphazard market-timing move, such as moving the whole portfolio into cash, can have long-lasting negative effects. Strong returns can be seen during the later stages of an economic cycle or may even happen right after the market hits its lowest. This is why all marketing gurus recommend the dollar-cost averaging method. This approach allows investors to buy shares cheaply as they wait for the market to rebound.

What Should You Do to Prepare for a Recession?

You can do many things to prepare for a recession, some of which will be discussed in detail in this book. Every investor must first stay calm and composed while looking at the market and think of long-term goals instead of focusing on immediate money. Emotions and markets do not mix well and may lead to heavy losses. This is especially true during hard times and market and economic stress periods.

As mentioned earlier, predicting the recession's beginning, middle, and the end is impossible. Not only is it impossible, but it is also not very critical. You can survive just about and perhaps earn profit without caring for these things. The more important thing is to have a long-term goal and point of view and keep your portfolio balanced. Be resilient and allow your portfolio to be the same. A volatile market should not make your mind volatile too.

If you have money during the recession, you can earn more by investing it properly.

Investing money to gain money can be easy- or it can be the most challenging thing you have ever done. Human psychology has a massive stake in how a person or people invest. Many people refrain from investing when they see the market going down and all the numbers turning red rapidly. When people see such figures, the first thing they do is hold their horses and keep their money safe with them. You will be surprised to know that this decision may be harmful in the long run.

In fact, keeping the money safe is perhaps the opposite thing you should do during such a period. If you want to make as much money as possible, the best way to do so is by investing money, albeit in an informed manner. Invest well, and you will see your money doubling. If you want to save money, the best time to do so is when the market is overperforming. This chapter will cover investing basics and similar decisions you should take during a recession.

If you think that recessions concern poor economic growth, then think again. Recessions are often associated and come along with a plethora of other problems, and these include low availability of jobs, a lot of job losses, and increased government relief.

Government relief may include increased unemployment benefits and stimulus payments. But all this does not mean that you should stop investing. If you are experiencing a recession in your region or can see one coming shortly, you may think about it and decide to invest. Before we begin, let us answer a fundamental question: Is investing safe during a recession?

The answer to this simple question is quite simple too. Yes, it is acceptable to invest during a recession. In fact, it can be your best investment to this day. During the recession, the stock values often go down quite significantly. While this may seem bad for any existing portfolio, you will be surprised to know that this wrong time can be turned into a good one by investing correctly.

Lower stock values can allow you an excellent opportunity to invest in a reasonably inexpensive manner. In such conditions, it is highly recommended to invest. But there are a few caveats or conditions that you must follow before you decide to invest.

Only invest if you have a lot of emergency savings. It is necessary to have a stock of money in your savings before you decide to spend a lot of it on investment. Ideally, it is recommended to have enough money in savings that would last for at least three to six months. The more, the better. If you do have extra money at your disposal, you can feel free to invest it by making good choices. If you do not have such an emergency fund, it is recommended to build a fund before you can start investing or doing anything.

Investments made during the recession are generally long-term investments. You won't be able to see your money or profits for at least seven years. Thus, if you want to invest during a recession, you should be more than willing to take a risk. It is not something meant for the faint of heart.

The market is rarely stable for a long time. You may buy at a low price and see it grow for a few days, only to see its value decrease in a few weeks. This is normal. But remember, the best way to avoid failure and losses during a recession is to invest for a longer term. Just invest and forget the money. You won't be seeing it for a long time, and it is futile to obsessively check your portfolio daily. However, you should check your brokerage account more regularly and keep track of your portfolio when there is a recession, or the economy is suffering.

The more you check your investments, the more you will panic. It will stress you out to see your investments and portfolio declining. But this will change with time. Panic and stress are bad for everyone, but they are especially bad for investors as they can lead to haphazard and rash decisions. You may end up putting your money in poorly performing stocks, ultimately leading to losses.

Investing during a recession can bring you a lot of profit, but you must be in an excellent position to do so. This means you need to be financially stable and should be willing to put in some money for a long time. You also need to have the correct approach and the right attitude. Without these two things, you are ultimately bound to suffer. Never compromise your financial stability and security for quick bucks- it will come to bite you back someday.

If you do not have enough money or investing may lead to a cash crunch, it is better to lose opportunities than take a step towards bankruptcy. Focus on your daily necessities and bills, and be mentally and physically healthy. Keep your mind and heart steady and wait for better opportunities, for they are sure to come. You can always make investments later in life when you are more secure and steady. Once your earnings are steady, you have a secure job, and your physical and mental health is good, you feel much better investing.

Data of Investment During Recessions

Data does not lie. Investing in long-term programs can really work and get you a lot of profit if done correctly. For instance, all significant recessions of recent times- Covid 19, the Great Recession of 2007, the dot-com crash, and the 1990-91 recession- have cases of long-term investors profiting immensely.

Investing during the market's lowest point may lead to massive profits later. The only thing you need to remember is to invest for a longer term. Remember that the market is unpredictable, and you never know when it will rise or decline. You may not find the best time to invest; however, you may still find a good time to invest if you are vigilant and quick. It does not matter if you do not find the best investment time; anything adjacent will do.

For instance, let us assume a person invested in an S & P 500 index fund around the worst time in the 2007 recession. This means you invested in the market's peak before it began to collapse. In such a case, over the past 13 years, you would have achieved around 8.4% profit. The same is the case with the 1990 recession, where you may have gained around 9.8% profit in the past 30 years.

In simpler words, let us assume you may have invested around $10000 in the 1990 recession. Over the years, your investment would have grown up to $150,000 in value. You should have invested the dividends from time to time.

What to Invest

The next chapter will cover this section in detail; however, here is a brief overview of all the investment possibilities you can consider during the recession.

Index funds are a fantastic investment- whether in recession or in regular times. You can purchase index funds, especially S&P 500 index funds, for the long term. This can be a fantastic investment over a long period.

This does not mean that you cannot invest in individual stocks. Many people prefer to invest in individual stocks. In such a case, it is better to find an environment or a bunch of exemplary businesses and stick to them. Stick to them as long as they are good businesses. This is a good tip, but it becomes essential during a recession.

For instance, during the COVID-19 pandemic and the resulting recession, many companies with solid balance sheets went into crisis. However, they had a better advantage than those that did not suffer too much. Companies with financial flexibility can survive long-term problems and are thus a great place to invest your money. On the other hand, companies with otherwise good businesses but low liquidity can hit the ground hard. Many such companies did not even survive the pandemic.

When investing during a recession, two things matter a lot: what you invest in and how you invest your capital. Stocks are generally quite volatile during a recession, which can be quite challenging. Instead of trying to time the market, investing in an incremental format is recommended. This strategy is known as dollar-cost averaging, which will be covered in detail in a subsequent chapter. This involves an investment of equal dollar amounts at timed intervals instead of a one-time purchase. Thus, you will be able to earn more profits if the prices continue to fall. If you see the prices fall, you can also buy a higher number of stocks for the same amount. Thus, a recession can ultimately be a fantastic time to buy stocks from big companies at cheap rates.

What Not to Invest in During a Recession

Recessions can be a boon and a curse for investors. It all depends on how and what you invest. Weak or small companies often go bankrupt during a recession, and for bigger companies, the stocks may go down by 80+% during recessions. But not all that is cheap is good. If the price of stocks of a company seems too good to be true, it is generally so.

Such companies might be on the verge of collapse. Just because you can buy stocks at dirt-cheap rates does not mean you should buy them. Ultimately, a dying business, whether cheap or expensive, is nothing more than a dying business itself.

There are certain factors that you must consider while investing during a recession. Some companies and investments are a strict no-no. Here are a few tips to get you started.

Don't Wait for the Right Time

Waiting for the right time, i.e., waiting for the time when the market will hit bottom, will lead to disastrous effects. It is a losing battle as the market is extremely volatile. Yes, investing during the bottom-most time of the market will earn the top-most profits, but if you wait for it, you may end up with nothing in your hand. Remember, never be greedy. Assessing when the market will hit bottom is like waiting and trying to play the lottery. Only one in millions will win it. Instead of waiting for the right time, invest in stocks or funds you would not mind holding for the long term. This means that even if the market falls, you will be safe.

Avoid Day Trading

Nowadays, it has become quite easy to trade thanks to the Internet. Furthermore, user-friendly apps and zero-commission stock trades have made investing akin to child's play. You may do day trading with a small sum of money you don't mind losing. But if you want to earn more profits with added stability, it is recommended to invest for longer terms. Day trading is generally a bad idea if you are unaware of the market and not an expert.

When and When Not to Sell

Many people quickly sell their stocks when they go down. This may seem obvious, but it is not the correct one. One thing that you must remember to avoid during a recession is to stop panicking if your stocks begin to fall. Volatile situations can be scary, but this does not mean that they won't change. Do not let your heart cloud your brain; do not let your emotions rule your judgment. Doing any transaction in a state of panic can lead to various problems. Often times you may sell stocks for lower than what you had purchased them for. This proves to be counterproductive to the principle of investing. To earn profit through investments, you need to sell stocks at a higher price than what you paid for them. This is a crucial factoid that must be remembered whenever you transact. The approach to investing during a recession should not be much different than investing during normal times. It is quite similar. Keep in mind that you should try to invest in high-quality companies or funds and hold on to these for the long term if possible.

How to Profit from the Recession

It is better to dig the well when the time is right instead of trying to dig it when you are thirsty. If you feel a recession is coming, staying calm and not worrying a lot is necessary. You are bound to feel the bite of this snake; barely anyone can escape it. They are inevitable and are generally never good news, but if you stay well prepared, you can come through them without facing many difficulties and perhaps even get a lot of profit. Here are some ways you can not only thrive and survive during the recession but perhaps even make a profit.

Hoard Cash During Normal Times

No, you do not need to become a scrooge, but it is still necessary to save some money to build capital that can then be invested during the recession for high profits. Many people panic and try to steer clear of stocks - unfortunately, at the wrong time. This is why many investors experience a worse rate of returns during the recession than the market itself. According to many examples, it is clear that investors should buy many different stocks, such as index mutual funds, and hold them for the long term. You can also rebalance the asset allocation from time to time. But the buy-and-hold strategy can be quite difficult. It may lead to a cash crunch and other similar issues. But you can avoid this by having a piggy bank with you.

Having a bank or a cash cushion during 'normal' times will allow you to invest safely. This amount can be invested as a lump sum during the recession, but to make the deal even sweeter, use the dollar-cost averaging method. This will ensure good profits.

Sometimes when you invest during a recession, the market, instead of getting better, continues to get worse. In such a case, instead of panicking, you should wait. The harder the market falls, the higher it will rise. Just be patient and wait.

Credits and Loans

Credit is a difficult thing to get during a recession. People tighten the strings of their purses, and you may find it difficult to access credit. In such times, it is better to have a good credit score and a better chance of getting a loan.

But why do you need a loan? Loans can be important for many personal as well as professional endeavors, but nowadays, people also tend to borrow so that they can invest. This can be a foolhardy method of earning profit and may throw you into the depths of bankruptcy.

Getting a good credit score does not happen immediately; you must work on it for a long time. Do not wait for the economy or the market to tank; start working on your credit score immediately. Ensure that it is in excellent health.

Investment in Real Estate

It is rare to find the housing market declining for a long time. Housing prices are generally higher than the sky, but with the recession, things might change.

People often delay their purchase of houses because they wait for the market to get better. This is a rookie mistake, as it rarely happens. You may never get a bargain on the house prices. The housing market is quite similar to the stock market. The housing market, like the stock market, rarely changes; in this case, rarely often means never.

If you are good enough and guess the right and fortunate time, you can purchase a house at a bargain price- if other prospective buyers cannot. The fewer prospective buyers, the more the chances of getting a good deal. Lower demand also lowers prices. This is why you should save cash to have a good amount for the down payment and jump at the opportunity immediately. Having a high down payment will bring down the expenses of the mortgage, but it will also reduce the amount you may have to borrow.

Planning

It is recommended to plan all your big expenses during a recession to utilize them later. Recessions hit everyone, and only a few are left untouched by them. Even the most successful businesses might collapse and look for new revenue and sales. This is true for small-time business owners too.

If you plan to do a major home renovation, saving money is recommended and utilizing it judiciously. You can hire contractors for a bargain price when the times are difficult. This same tip can apply to big-ticket purchases. For instance, car dealerships are often ready to sell their ware at lower rates during the recession when the sales are slow and low. Such businesses are often ready to cut the prices just so that they get customers and, in turn, money.

Career Changes: an Investment of Time

Most employees around the world hate their job or even their careers. Such employees are often forced to stay in their job just because their position is stable and they are getting good money. But this does not mean that you should stop dreaming. Instead of worrying, start thinking about better things. Try to find out more about new career paths until you find something that suits your tastes, desires, and pay scale.

If your job needs additional training or certificates, start working on them now. You can find local schools' training, or you can even learn online.

Not many companies are looking to hire new people during a recession. But try to ride the wave and go back and learn more to prepare for a better job and an amazing future. With luck, you will be able to get a better job once the recession begins to fade.

Chapter Two: Invest in Safe Companies

The market becomes extremely volatile during a recession, which may lead to companies filing for bankruptcy everywhere. Generally, these are small-sized companies that cease to make a profit, but in extreme conditions, the same fate may befall bigger and stable companies too. Yet, investing in fairly stable companies is much better than choosing a not-so-stable company.

Ideally, it is better to avoid companies that may take a lot of time to recover or may not recover. Focus on large companies that have the potential to grow in the future. Such companies may have had historically low valuations, but it does not matter if they have enough potential to grow in the long term.

Generally, high-risk companies often decline and plummet during a recession. As it is impossible to predict the future, some companies may thrive and survive the crash, but choosing something with no or a very low chance of bankruptcy is still better. Investors often move from high-risk stocks to low-risk stocks during a recession. This often leads to a further declination of high-risk stocks, making them even more susceptible to crashes.

Thus, it is always better to look for companies performing well, even during recessions. The best place to invest in such a time is in low-cost supermarkets. This is a good option, as most of the population would be looking to cut food costs during a recession. This chapter will focus on various methods of making money during a recession and how you can become a smart investor to gain more profit during a recession.

Making Money in a Recession

During a recession, there are extreme economic hardships, and companies either cut down on their staff or may completely plummet. This is a time when the stock market also suffers, and stock prices drop to lower values. But this does not mean you cannot earn money and profit during and after a recession. It is recommended to indulge in renting and selling things that you own to get more profit. This profit can then be invested to get more profit. But the investment needs to be judicious. If you have enough capital, you can make smart and judicious investments that can then be turned into profit during and after a recession. Here are a few tried and tested methods you may employ during a recession to earn profit.

Government Bonds

Surprised right? Yes, government bonds are the safest ways to invest your money. If you have some capital and are trying to find a place where you can invest safely and see them grow during a recession, then government bonds are your friends. It is a great starting place for all new investors. Bonds are often considered to be a safe option of investment, even during times when other investment options are considered to be unstable and volatile. It has been observed that the value of Government bonds often goes up during recessions. While there are many different options to consider, many people prefer to invest in United States Treasury Bonds or USTB. The official website will give you a lot of information on this bond to make an informed decision.

Invest When Prices Are Down

If you have stable employment and your income has not gone down during the recession, you can choose to make good investment decisions that can be used to make a profit and more money. It is similar to making the most of the situation when the stock market has declined, and stock prices are very low. Once the economy improves, you can gain a huge profit margin when you invest in stocks during this recession time.

There is a lot of evidence that investing in diversified stock during a US recession can generate a huge profit. It can earn you a lot of profit- if you are ready to wait. Stock is volatile and inconsistent in the short run, but you will see it rising immensely if you are patient enough. While predicting the stock market is impossible, you can try to be patient and see for yourself how your ratio of profit rises.

Investing in Precious Metals

This may sound outdated to some, but such people are misguided. Investing in gold, silver, or any precious metal is very lucrative during recessions. The prices of precious metals often go up compared to other assets during the recession. While there is no guarantee that all your investments will produce profit, investing in something stable is still better than choosing something risky. Big risks lead to bigger profits, but similarly, bigger risks can also lead to humongous losses.

Invest in Retirement Savings

Many people choose to invest in retirement savings during a recession. This is a good time to increase your 401(k) contribution. Any funds invested in 401

(K) or retirement savings can also profit you by increasing your purchasing power. As soon as the recession ends, you will see the value of the assets in your portfolio go up. The value of your investments in your retirement savings will also go up.

Lend Money

This may seem morally wrong, but it can be quite a good investment opportunity. If you have cash on hand and are looking to get a good investment but do not want to invest in the stock market, it is recommended to lend the money to people in need. You can become an individual moneylender. Peer-to-peer money lending has become a huge business in recent times. Many websites can serve as a medium between lenders and borrowers to cut a lot of documentation and red tape.

Do remember that this can be a risky choice. It depends on you how much and to whom to lend. Risky investments or similar lending may lead to humongous losses, so beware and be safe. You can lend to either businesses or individuals. Average returns of lending can be anywhere between 6% and 8%.

Invest in Real Estate

Recessions can be quite a great situation to invest in properties as the rates of properties or real estate often go down during such periods. When the market is more stable, and there is growth, such properties can be sold at a good profit. The properties don't necessarily have to be "turned" either. They can be sold without spending any money on refurbishment. To assess a fair price, always check the current housing market. This is recommended when you buy or even sell a property. It will help you get the best deal possible and also allow you to get a good profit later.

You may also want to be prepared to jump on a property if you see a good deal. This may include a pre-approved mortgage, and you may take the help of a dedicated home inspector. Be quick and cautious; otherwise, you may lose the deal.

Always be on the lookout for sellers desperate to sell their properties. They often have bargain-price, and you can buy the property for dirt-cheap. Sellers often are in a better position than buyers in such cases.

Always look for a good and trustworthy lawyer when you are looking to purchase a property. A good lawyer will do a title search on the property to check its details. This will help ensure that you don't buy any property with liens. If you skip this step, you may buy a property where you owe money to a contractor or lender.

Selling and Renting to Make Money

Renting Out a Place

If you have your own house and are willing to take on a stranger to live with you, renting out a place during a recession can be a great way to profit. A property is one of a person's most significant assets, and you can turn it into money. One of the most straightforward ways to make money is by renting out one or as many extra rooms as you have in your home. It will generate a monthly rental income and help you reduce your spending on mortgage repayment. You can contact a real estate agent to help find tenants or just post openings yourself. It will also help you save on utility bills and taxes.

You can rent a room on your own or contact an estate agent to do so. While independent renting will save you brokerage, going through the medium of a real estate agent may provide you more protection and security. It is necessary to vet potential housemates carefully and thoroughly. If you can, try to get references from their previous landlords and their jobs.

If you do not want to rent your property for a long time, you can also rent it for a few days using web services such as HomeAway and Airbnb. These websites will also charge mediator fees, allowing you to find a higher number of tenants- semi-permanent and temporary. This will also allow you to find flexible tenants so that you get to enjoy your own space whenever you want.

Rent Out Parking Space

While the number of privately owned vehicles is rising, parking or the lack of parking has become a grave problem. For people with their own parking spaces in big cities, an easy way to supplement income is by renting the space out. A parking space can be a surprisingly lucrative asset. The area you live in or own the parking spot in will determine how much you can charge for this service. Areas near commercial centers, train stations, or anywhere with a lot of regular activity will usually generate higher rent than suburban areas.

However, it is important to check the terms and conditions for your parking permit first. If you end up allowing illegal parking, you may have to pay a very heavy fine. Once you have confirmed that it is okay to rent out the space, you will be able to advertise your parking space online.

Sell Things

While very few of us are hoarders, we often tend to have a plethora of things that are either unused, unwanted or of no use to us anymore. Selling these things online or online can be a good way to profit during a recession. This can include anything- right from expensive jewelry to old clothes and pieces of furniture. During a recession, people are more likely to buy used items than in normal times.

You can use various auction sites like eBay and others to sell things. You can also use more special and niche sites, including Etsy, to sell things that you believe will fetch more prices than what they get on eBay. Instead of putting all your eggs in one basket, consider listing your items on multiple sites. But do remember to take off the listings once the product has been sold.

Instead of jumping into the selling business right away, try to research and find out how to get the most profit. You can check out similar items on sites like eBay and Amazon to find more details.

Do not lie or hide things. Be as truthful and accurate while selling things and describe them so. Click good pictures of your products, as they will help you sell them off quicker.

Sell Offline

If you do not want to sell your things online or want to supplement your online sales, you can do so through second-hand stores and local thrift stores. Most store owners will be more than happy to buy things from you. Always meet the storeowners face-to-face and explain your items' details. If your items are small, you can also carry them with you so that they can appraise them and provide you with a good price point. This does require a lot of legwork, but on the other hand, it will save you a lot of time listing things online.

You can either choose to sell the products right away or can also choose the option of consignment. In the case of consignment, you will receive a previously agreed-upon percentage of the sale. This means you will have to wait until the product is sold. If you need money immediately, you can sell it outright.

Second-hand stores can pay huge sums for pieces of furniture and vintage apparel, and jewelry.

Instead of selling or cracking a deal with the first shop, you enter, move around and try out more shops. Try to find out your goods' average price point before you sell.

Certain shops that generally do not deal in second-hand goods may also be willing to buy used goods. These include sports shops, bookshops, jewelry shops, etc.

Supplement Your Investment to Gain More Capital

These tips can be used to raise capital, which can be invested to earn high profits.

Tutoring

Tutoring is an easy way to get some cash during a recession. Finding any job prospects or employment during a recession is quite difficult. This is because employers are often trying to get rid of staff instead of looking to expand. If you see that you are struggling to make money or are looking to increase your capital for investment, tutoring in your spare time can help you. Tutoring is a productive way of using your knowledge and skills to gain money and experience. You do not have to do it every day; you can get extra money by tutoring on weekends, evenings, or even on your off days.

Many different avenues fall under the umbrella of tutoring. One common avenue is tutoring. You can tutor kids after their school hours and can help them with their exam preparations. Other than this, many other tutoring options will allow you to use your expertise and knowledge and help you make more money. For instance, musicians can take music lessons for beginners. People who are fluent in a foreign language can tutor someone interested in that language. Many people also like signing up for cooking or baking classes. So if you are good at any such supplementary activities, you can take lessons for adults or kids. If you are good at driving, you can also sign up as an instructor. You may, however, need to take a few certification exams for certain jobs like the latter.

Mystery Shopping

Mystery shopping has become a popular pastime thanks to the boom in online shopping. You can get some extra bucks through mystery shopping on evenings and weekends. These things do not produce a lot of cash, but they are quite easy to do. You can find many opportunities for mystery shopping online. Just be sure to make an informed choice and that you do not choose any random listing thrown at you.

Mystery shopping is simple; you just need to go to a business, a service provider, or a store and ask questions about a particular service or product or buy something. Then you have to jot down the details in a prescribed form. These details may include your experience in the store, your experience with customer service, etc.

This field is plagued with scams, and if you are not careful, you may lose your time and, in extreme cases, your money. Do not pay any heed to companies that seem 'scammy.' This also includes companies that charge a membership fee or any other similar charges. Never pay any fees and never respond to any unsolicited emails or messages. Such messages are generally scams.

Online Surveys

Another way of getting some cash and building your capital for investment is by taking online surveys. This is an easy and quick way to get some cash that you can do in your own time and space. But this will not give you a lot of money, and it may take some time before you can collect a considerable amount. Generally, a five-ten minute survey pays a couple of dollars.

The best thing about these surveys is that they are more or less never affected by the recession and are convenient enough to do in your spare time.

Before choosing any platform:

- Try to find some information regarding websites offering forms and compare their terms, conditions, and rates.

- Do not sign up without having a thorough run of the details of these companies.

- Never commit to a company without checking with their past employees. For instance, certain companies do not pay in cash but in vouchers.

Use Apps to Make Money

Smartphones have changed the way we live and look at the world. They are not only a way to stay connected with people but also to create, enjoy, and relax. But smartphones can also be used to make money. Many apps available in the market can be used to make some extra cash. These apps are easy, quick, and do not take much time.

While these apps do not provide much money, thanks to their quickness, you will surely be able to collect a considerable amount of money in no time. The requirements of the apps you need to fulfill to get money vary. For instance, certain apps ask you to fill out quick surveys; some ask you to click pictures of your receipts, some ask you to check the prices of certain products, and some may ask you to watch specific videos.

Some revolutionary apps also offer you money just to install them. Many apps will collect anonymous stats from your phone to create a profile for targeted ads. This includes what websites you frequent, how long you spend on these websites, basic personal details, etc.

Certain apps can also provide you cash rewards for guessing the outcome of a sporting event.

Be a Private Cab Driver

If you have a vehicle of your own, you can use it as a private cab and earn lots of money. Uber and other similar services allow you to use your car as a cab.

You just need to sign up on the website and fill up certain forms, data related to your car, your personal details, etc. once this is done, you just have undergone a background check, and in no time, you will be able to drive people around to earn cash.

Complete Odd Jobs

There are many odd jobs that you can do online as well as offline to get some extra cash. These are generally short tasks that do not take a lot of time— most of these things you can do from the leisure of your home. Freelancers have a lot of options to try out. You can test websites, transcribe audio files, translate text documents, and more. If you are skilled at something or have a productive hobby, try making it a business and turn profits.

There are a lot of websites online these days catering to freelancers. Some examples include Freelancer, Guru, Fiverr, Upwork, TopTal, etc.

In the initial days, you may not get much money from such gigs, but once you become established, you will be surprised to see how much you can make through freelancing.

Beware, there exist many scams that may dig a hole in your bank account. Only sign up to work with trustworthy and established websites and apps.

Chapter Three: Dollar Cost Averaging

As repeated earlier, it is quite difficult or almost impossible to time the market, as it is a volatile entity. In such cases, the best way to sustain and perhaps gain profit is to divide your investment into multiple periods. Instead of investing one single time, try to do it several times. This way, you won't worry about the bottom of the market or its peak.

Investing in undervalued companies that are secure and have the potential to grow is recommended. This will allow you to succeed with time- if you are patient. An easy way to do this is by putting considerable funds in a kitty and passing it on to your broker. Once this is done, choose a couple of days each month (or every alternate month) and ask your broker to invest in 5-10 stocks accordingly.

Choose stocks you feel won't fall and will grow once the recession ends. It does not matter if the valuation of these companies goes down. If you trust the company to rise again, continue investing in it. This method removes the negative implications of the human psyche associated with investing.

Investing in Dollar Cost Averaging

This method is used by investors worldwide who want to invest but not in one lump sum. This method works great for how much you may invest at one time. Another factor that makes this method good for almost all investors is that it reduces the risks associated with investing as a lump sum. In this method, the investor purchases multiple shares over a period of time instead of buying them altogether. It does not matter what the price of the shares is. Dollar-cost averaging is highly recommended for beginner investors and can make your investment prices go down and enhance your profits.

What Is Dollar Cost Averaging?

As the market is volatile, prices are not linear or unidirectional; they can change rapidly. Just divide your money carefully and invest judiciously. Over time you are bound to see profits.

Market Timing and Dollar Cost Averaging: the Difference

Dollar-cost averaging works on the principle that the costs of assets go up over the long term. The prices of assets are unpredictable, just like the market. They may not go up consistently and may experience many highs and lows. There is no established pattern for them.

People often purchase assets when the prices are low. While this is easy on paper, it is notoriously difficult in practice. It is not only difficult but rather impossible to assess and time market, and even professionals cannot do it successfully. It is possible that a stock that is going down today may suddenly begin to rise the very next day. Unless you are Nostradamus and can make prophecies, it is better to avoid trying to predict the market anyway.

You may analyze the market later once it has changed. But this retrospective knowledge cannot be used to predict the coming market movement. If you sit and try to analyze the market, you have most likely lost the right opportunity to invest. Do not be on the sidelines and take the jump. Just try to stay afloat.

Trying to time the market is useless and may even lead to heavy losses. Such people often have little to no profit.

The Workings of Dollar Cost Averaging Explained

Dollar-cost averaging takes away the stress and emotions from investing. It allows investors to invest a small but regular amount at regular intervals.

For example, you may invest $2400 in a fund as a lump sum. You will regularly invest $200 monthly in the dollar cost averaging method.

While both these approaches may seem the same in theory, in the long term, it can be observed that dollar cost averaging may produce more profit than any other method. You may be able to purchase more shares using this method than you would have if you had invested as a lump sum.

Helps People Who Have Less to Invest

Dollar-cost averaging is a good method for new investors as it allows them to start slowly with less money and risks.

Many people don't have access to ready funds at all times. For such people, dollar cost averaging works. Through this method, they can invest in the market at constant intervals. You don't even need to wait to collect the capital. Just start investing and keep the schedule up.

Dollar-cost averaging involves regular investments. This means the investor can continue to invest even if the market is down. It can be quite a daunting experience to continue investing when the market dips.

Is Dollar Cost Averaging a Good Option?

Hypothetically, dollar cost averaging should work every time. But as the market is quite unstable, this is not always the case. According to certain independent surveys, lump sum investments may produce better results and profits than dollar cost averaging.

If you are okay with investing in a lump sum, you can go ahead and do so. But if you are worried about the risks, you should choose dollar-cost investing instead.

The results of this research are unstable and may change according to the individual. For instance, people who do not have a lot of money on hand or don't want to invest as a lump sum amount can use dollar cost averaging. This will allow them to earn profits and stay in the market.

The psychological stress of investing a lump sum amount, especially if you are a beginner, is massive. People who are prone to anxiety should avoid it. Such people are recommended to use dollar cost averaging instead.

Dollar-cost averaging has its own pros and cons. It can ultimately help you earn profit and make your money grow. In some cases, the profits might be lower than what you would have if you had invested as a lump sum, but if you compare the risks, dollar cost averaging is still the winner.

In many cases, dollar cost averaging can produce more profit than investing as a lump sum amount.

Predicting the market accurately is not easy. It is recommended to avoid making such predictions using dollar cost averaging.

Who Should Use Dollar Cost Average?

All investors can use dollar cost averaging, but it is especially recommended for the following people:

- You do not have a large kitty and cannot or don't want to invest as a lump sum.

- You are a beginner.

- You are looking to invest in 401 (k), an IRA, or other similar retirement accounts.

- You don't know how to do market timing research.

- You know how to research market timing but do not want to do it.

- You are apprehensive about investing in a down market.

It is better to invest using other strategies if:

- You are an experienced investor and have been investing for a long time.

- You understand the market well.

- You have a big kitty you would like to invest in as a lump sum.

- You prefer to invest in mutual funds. Generally, investing in mutual funds requires a higher minimum investment.

- You like timing the market and are aware of how to do it.

- You do not want to invest for a longer term.

How to Invest During a Recession

It does not matter if the next recession will be mild or harsh; it is recommended to structure and plan their portfolios carefully to avoid losses and gain profit.

Cash

When the economy becomes unstable, cash becomes the sole emperor. It is always recommended to stock up on cash reserves when the employment rate is high. This way, you will have good capital to invest during the recession.

This does not mean you should sell your investments just because you think a recession is coming. Investors often give away their stocks in a hurry and then realize their mistake once the market starts to ascend. Instead, divert the money into well-positioned and stable investments. This is why keeping a chunk of your portfolio into liquid securities or hard cash is necessary.

Purchase Good Assets in the Time of a Recession

Investing in good and quality assets is necessary for the investor's portfolio to stay stable and secure. A quality asset has low beta, leverage, and high returns.

Such quality asset companies are called evergreen businesses. Unlike many other companies, they are not as heavily dependent on economic growth for their growth or survival. Companies with a big recurring stream of revenue, like subscription-based models, will often handle recessions a lot better.

Look into a company's debt load and refrain from investing in those with high debt. These companies are bound to fail at any time. They may find it difficult to pay off their debt if their income declines.

Avoid Growth Stocks

If you believe that a recession is on the horizon, then stop investing in growth stocks immediately. Companies with no profit margin and are assumed to grow in the future fail immediately during a recession. Instead, try to focus on other investment ventures, such as dividend-paying stocks.

Bonds and Uncorrelated Assets

An investor can invest in bonds during a recession if they are investment-grade bonds. These include carbon credits, insurance-linked securities, and similar asset classes.

Invest in Dividend Stocks

Dividend stocks are highly profitable during a recession. They can provide a good backup plan during a recession. They continue to be profitable even if the companies' stock prices go down. They are closely related to dollar cost averaging.

This makes them very important when the market is undergoing a lot of volatility.

Actively Managed Funds

Investors should consider investing in actively managed funds during a recession. Research shows that these actively managed funds tend to do better than others by almost 5% annually. This is an average after risk and expense adjustments are made.

Avoid Overreaction during a Recession

No one can predict a recession. But if you can sense that we may go through a period of economic downfall, it is recommended to stay calm. Continuing your investment practices and following the same during a recession is the recommended way to go.

Recessions can be difficult for growing wealth and returns; remember that the market is always looking forward. The best way to earn profits is to invest completely and not be scared by short-term market movements. Stay focused on your long-term goal, and you are bound to succeed.

Glossary of Financial Terms

This glossary will serve as a quick guide for various financial concepts. While many other financial terms are equally important, this glossary can serve as a beginning point from which you can delve into the world of economics more nuancedly.

A

AAA - Triple A rating. This is the highest rating a fund or a financial instrument can get. Various independent rating agencies check it.

B

Bad Debt - A defaulted debt or debt with little to no hope of getting repaid.

Bear Market - A market going down.

Bubble - A condition in which prices are inflated artificially, overly, or both. The inflation does not correspond to supply and demand.

Bull Market - A market going up.

C

Commodities - All raw goods that are traded on the market.

D

Deflation - Opposite of inflation, prices go down.

Depression - First used by president Franklin D Roosevelt. Economists picked up the term, and now it has become a part of the financial lexicon. A period of extreme poverty.

G

Global Recession - When the global GDP growth is lower than 3%.

GDP (Gross Domestic Product) - The total value of all services and goods made in a country minus the differential between imports and exports. It is different from GNP or Gross National Product as the latter also includes a differential between finances had abroad by Americans and finances made in America by non-Americans.

P

Pyramid/Ponzi Scheme - A fraudulent financial scheme in which the manager gets new investors to pay off the older ones. This term comes from Charles Ponzi, an Italian American financier who was a well-known scamster.

R

Recession – If a negative economic growth or economic decline is observed for two or more consecutive quarters, such a period is known as recession.

S

Security - An umbrella term that includes financial instruments that can be purchased and sold. This includes bonds, stocks, futures, and options.

U

US Treasury - This is the bank that handles the funds of the US government. It is often used to represent the US Department of Treasury, which holds the power of printing paper currency and managing federal revenue. You can find out more about this online on the official website.

Conclusion

Recessions are difficult for everyone, especially if you are unfamiliar with the market and new to investing. But recessions can also prove a boon for investors if they know where, when, and how to invest. This book has been written as a brief guide for such people who want to learn more about investing and how they can earn profit and capital for investing during a recession.

They say that one should make hay when the sun is shining. But in the case of recession, investors should make hay or money when the economy's sun is setting. It can be an extremely rewarding experience to invest during a recession, which can even help you get ahead in life.

People avoid investing during a recession because the 'red numbers' scare them. But remember, the bigger the risk, the better the profits. Dare to take the leap and invest; you will surely succeed.

The methods given in this book have been tried and tested and have historically worked. However, as it is impossible to time and predict the market, it is still recommended to think carefully and plan strategically before you decide to invest.

Invest now and take a step towards a golden future.

References

6 Things You Must Do When Your Savings Reach $250,000. (2022, September 14). Money Talks News. https://www.moneytalksnews.com/6-things-you-must-do-when-your-savings-reach-250000/

A recession glossary. (2009, May 21). France 24. https://www.france24.com/en/20090521-recession-glossary-

Frankel, M. (2020, April 26). Is It Safe to Invest During a Recession? The Motley Fool. https://www.fool.com/investing/how-to-invest/what-to-invest-in-recession/

Franz, J., & Spence, D. (2022, September 15). Preparing for the next recession: 9 things you need to know. Capital Group. https://www.capitalgroup.com/advisor/insights/articles/guide-to-recessions.html

Hicks, C. (2022, September 12). How To Invest During A Recession – Forbes Advisor. Www.forbes.com. https://www.forbes.com/advisor/investing/how-to-invest-during-a-recession/

Napoletano, E. (2020, August 6). How To Invest with Dollar Cost Averaging. Forbes Advisor. https://www.forbes.com/advisor/investing/dollar-cost-averaging/

Packard, B. (2022, September 14). 3 Ways to Make Money During a Recession. WikiHow. https://www.wikihow.com/Make-Money-During-a-Recession

Printed in Great Britain
by Amazon

27147360R00030